Handmade Tales

HANDMADE TALES

Stories to Make and Take

Dianne de Las Casas

Illustrated by Philip Chow

LIBRARIES UNLIMITED

A Member of the Greenwood Publishing Group

Westport, Connecticut • London

Library of Congress Cataloging-in-Publication Data

De Las Casas, Dianne.
Handmade tales : stories to make and take / Dianne de Las Casas ; illustrated by Philip Chow.
    p. cm.
  Includes bibliographical references and index.
  ISBN 978–1–59158–536–7 (alk. paper)
  1. Storytelling. 2. Children's libraries—Activity programs. I. Chow, Philip. II. Title.
  Z718.3.D43 2008
  027.62'51—dc22   2007033857

British Library Cataloguing in Publication Data is available.

Library of Congress Catalog Card Number: 2007033857
ISBN-13: 978-1-59158-536-7

First published in 2008

Libraries Unlimited, 88 Post Road West, Westport, CT 06881
A Member of the Greenwood Publishing Group, Inc.
www.lu.com

Printed in the United States of America

The paper used in this book complies with the
Permanent Paper Standard issued by the National
Information Standards Organization (Z39.48–1984).

10 9 8 7 6 5 4 3 2

For Johnette Downing
Who is, hands down, the best friend ever!
—Dianne de Las Casas

For Anita
Thank you for your support and understanding
—Philip Chow

Contents

Acknowledgments

I am certainly not the first to combine storytelling and handmade props. There are so many storytellers who came before me, to whom I owe a debt of gratitude for paving the way—Gale Criswell, Caroline Feller Bauer, Hiroko Fujita, Valerie Marsh, Anne Pellowski, Barbara Schutzgruber, Fran Stallings, David Titus, and many others. *Handmade Tales* was a labor of love and many years in the making. I have so many people to thank for helping me through the process.

A special thank you to the following people:

Antonio, Soleil and Eliana—For endless hours of listening and watching my various versions of the handmade tales. A special thank you to Soleil for modeling for many of the illustrations. I love you all times infinity.

Sharon Coatney (my awesome editor)—For always being open and receptive to my ideas. You are a doll!

Karen Chace—For sharing "The Snowflake Story" with me, for your countless hours of devotion to the storytelling community, and for being my friend.

Philip Chow—For spending hours on end perfecting the complex illustrations in this book. I am eternally grateful for your dedication and talent.

Gale Criswell—For your support and encouragement throughout the years. Thank you for teaching me "The Snooks Family," for inspiring my balloon tale, and for being there for the creation of the first handmade tale!

Johnette Downing—For being my "Title Queen" and best friend. You rock!

Louisiana librarians—For listening to my tales year after year. I love y'all!

Kat Mincz—For being my number one fan and cheerleader. I wrote "Catching a Pest" for you.

Mom, Clay, Gary and the James Kids—For listening to and loving my stories. I love you!

Introduction

As a child, I was always fascinated with making things by hand. As an adult, that childlike curiosity still burns inside. Since I love telling stories and I love making things by hand, I began experimenting on how to combine the two. That was the initial spark for *Handmade Tales*.

My first handmade tale was "Joseph Had An Overcoat." I was working with Gale Criswell, presenting a series of summer reading workshops for the State Library of Louisiana. Our theme was "Silly Chilly Summer," so I developed "Joseph Had an Overcoat" based on Simm Taback's picture book, *Joseph Had a Little Overcoat*. It was an immediate hit with the librarians and I knew I had to develop more handmade tales.

So I began exploring the different ways simple props made from common household items could be used to enhance storytelling. First, I started with cut and tell tales. I added draw and tell tales and string stories. Then I began asking myself, "What else can I use?" I was inspired by restaurant napkin folding, cruise line towel folding, folk toy making, and origami. Just take a look around. Inspiration abounds! Perhaps you'll be moved to create your own handmade tales.

The stories I have created range from very simple to complex. There are stories to share with preschoolers and elementary-age children. Even older students enjoy handmade tales. I love the magical moment when a simple piece of paper, string, or cloth is transformed and kids respond with, "Awesome!" Middle school and high school students love learning how to make handmade tales, so consider hosting a handmade tale workshop at your library or school.

In fact, these stories work for all ages. Handmade tales are great for home, classroom, and library settings. They even work on-the-go! Pack a string, bandana, and a small pair of scissors to create stories when all else fails. Don't be afraid to repeat a story. Kids will ask for these tales again and again until they begin mastering the handmade tales themselves. My six-year-old daughter loves "The Worm" (a string story) and "Papa's Teepee" (a cut and tell story) and tells it to the amazement of adults and children alike.

The great thing about handmade tales is that the visual elements of the stories help tellers remember the tales. Don't be intimidated by the combined aspects of storytelling and managing manipulatives. Here's a "handy" tip. First, learn the tale until you can tell it without thinking about it. Then learn the handmade technique until you can do it with your eyes closed. Finally, marry the story with the manipulative. Before you know it, you will master *Handmade Tales* and have stories you can make and take!

I'd love to hear how you are using *Handmade Tales*. Email me at dianne@storyconnection.net. We're going to have a great time so let's get started. Happy handmade tales to you!

Warmly,
Dianne de Las Casas

Part I

String Stories

The Pesky Skeeter

Create Mosquito string figure.

1. Loop string around both thumbs.

Start by looping the string
around your thumbs.

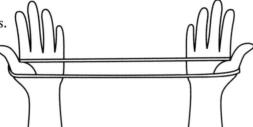

2. Pull the string around the back of your left hand. It should still be looped around each thumb.

Wrap the string around the
back of your left hand. It is
still looped around each
thumb.

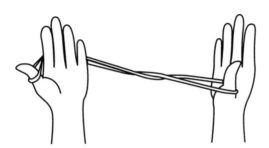

3. Reach across with your right pinkie and pull the strings between the left thumb and index finger.

Reach across with your right
pinkie and pick up both pieces
of string that run between your
thumb and first finger.

Pull your hands apart.

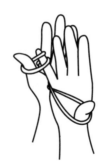

4. Pull your hands apart.

Now reach over all the strings
with your left pinkie and pick
up the two strings that come
off your right thumb.

Pull your hands apart.

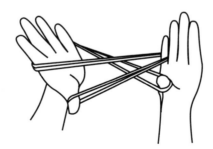

5. With your left pinkie, reach over all the strings and pull the two strings in front of the thumb and pull hands apart. Keep the loop around the thumb.

Squeeze the fingers of your left hand together to hold all the strings together. Use your right hand to pick up the strings that run around the back of your left hand. Pull them up over your fingers and drop them in front of your hand.

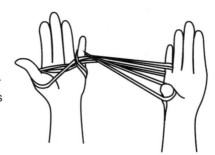

6. Keep your left fingers together and bend them down. With your right hand, pull the strings from behind the left hand over the fingers. Drop them in front of your hand.

Pull your hands apart and you'll see the mosquito. Wiggle your pinkies and thumbs in and out to make the mosquito fly. Don't forget to buzz like a mosquito as you do this.

7. Gently pull your hands apart and you should see the mosquito.

Now comes the good part. As soon as your audience admires your nicely buzzing mosquito, slap your hands together and shout "Got it!" Then pull your hands apart, letting the loops slip off of both pinkies. The mosquito will disappear.

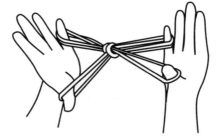

Story:

There once was a pesky skeeter. Create string figure quickly and show audience.

He saw a little girl and he wanted to eat her! Find a girl or woman in the audience and buzz mosquito over her head. Make a slurping sound.

He buzzed up and down. Buzz Mosquito up and down.

He buzzed all around. Buzz Mosquito over the top of audience members' heads.

Suddenly, he caught the little girl's eye. The little girl went POW! Clap hands together, releasing loops from the pinky fingers.

And the skeeter went bye bye! Pull your hands apart. Mosquito will disappear. Wave bye with one hand as you say, "bye bye!"

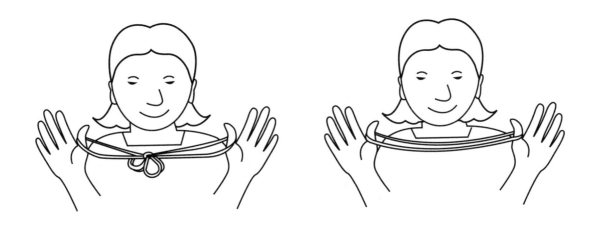

Fox Chases Bunny
A Shoestring Story

There was once a hungry fox. All he could think about was eating … Bunny!

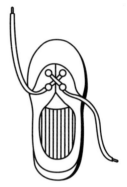

There was once a frightened Bunny. All she could think about was hiding from … Fox!

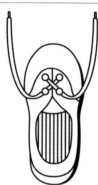

One day, Fox spied Bunny. He chased her around the lake. But he didn't catch Bunny.

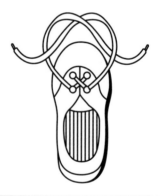

He chased her around a tree. But he didn't catch Bunny.

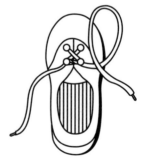

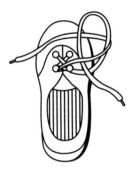

Bunny was so frightened that she ran so fast, she ran around the fox!

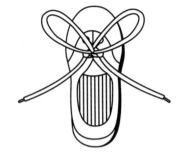

She ran all the way to her bunny burrow (that's a rabbit hole) and ran right in.

Fox chased her but guess what? He didn't catch Bunny.

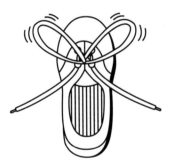

To this day, before Bunny goes out for the day, she pokes her head out of her bunny burrow to see if Fox is around. If you happen to pass by a bunny burrow, you just might see Bunny's ear twitching as she stays on the lookout for Fox!

The Worm

I love string stories. You can "string along" your audiences, who will be fascinated by the transformation. String stories do take a bit of practice. The story for this string figure is simple. My six-year-old learned to deliver it flawlessly! Once you master this story, you can move on to The Stubborn Turnip, which has essentially the same moves but a more complex story.

There once was a worm who liked to squirm. [Once string is on hand, swing from side to side as if squirming.]

With your left palm facing out, loop the string around your hand, including your thumb.

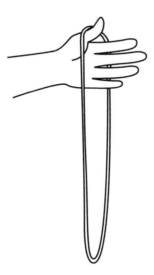

Into the garden dirt he'd go.

Using the index finger of your right hand, reach under the front string between the thumb and index finger of the left hand and pull a loop of the back string to the front as shown. Give the loop one clockwise twist and hook it over the left index finger. Remember the clockwise twist or the trick at the end will not work. Pull the loose ends of the string to tighten.

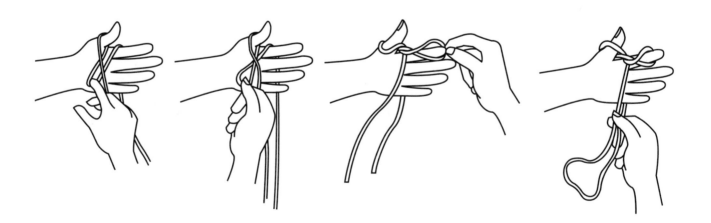

To help the plants and flowers grow.

Now, it's a matter of repeating the step. With your right index finger, reach under the front string between the index and middle finger, and pull a loop of the back string to the front under the top string. Give it a clockwise twist and hook the loop around the left middle finger. Pull the loose ends of the string to tighten. Advanced move: To perform the "grow" part of the story, release the loop from your left thumb and, with your right hand, pull it up. Then reloop the string around the thumb, as before, and tug on the bottom string to bring it back in place.

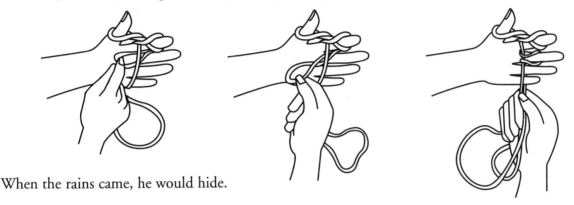

When the rains came, he would hide.

Repeat the step. With your right index finger, reach under the front string between the middle and ring finger, and pull a loop of the back string to the front under the top string. Give it a clockwise twist and hook the loop around the left ring finger. Tighten strings.

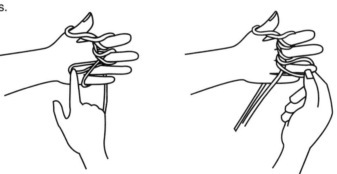

When the sun shone, he came back outside.

Repeat the step. With your right index finger, reach under the front string between the ring and pinkie finger, and pull a loop of the back string to the front under the top string. Give it a clockwise twist and hook the loop around the left pinkie finger.

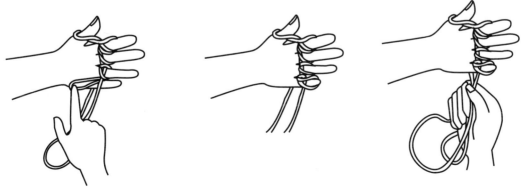

One day, he came out to take a peek.

Release loop from the thumb and allow it to stick up. This is the worm's head.

Worm saw a big bird with a giant beak!

With your right hand, grab the dangling string at the bottom and form into a large circle to symbolize big bird. Advanced move: Form a head and a beak with the string by creating a figure eight. One of the loops of the eight should be larger for the head. The other loop will be the beak.

So as quickly as he came, he squirmed away

To make the worm disappear, pull the long front string down. All the strings should unloop, releasing the entire string figure.

Now he stays in his hole to this very day.

Loop strings around both hands and stretch out, to make a big hole.

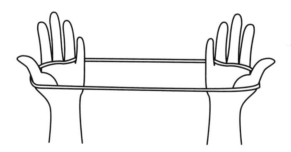

The Stubborn Turnip
A String Tale based on a Russian Folktale

Ma Farmer was in the garden and she saw that her turnip had grown to a giant size. She knew it was ready to pull. So she grabbed the turnip and she began to pull.

With your left palm facing out, loop the string around your hand, including your thumb. When you say, "She tried to pull it up" and "The stubborn turnip," tug on the string hanging down.

She tried to pull it up (clap, clap). She tried to pull it up (clap, clap).
The stubborn turnip (clap, clap). The stubborn turnip (clap, clap).

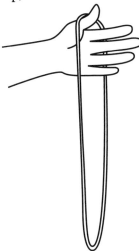

"That's a stubborn turnip," said Ma Farmer. She needed help so she called Pa Farmer. Pa grabbed Ma. Ma grabbed the turnip and they began to pull.

Using the index finger of your right hand, reach under the front string between the thumb and index finger of the left hand and pull a loop of the back string to the front as shown. Give the loop one clockwise twist and hook it over the left index finger. Remember the clockwise twist or the trick at the end will not work. Point to the corresponding fingers when you say "pa" and "ma." When you say, "She tried to pull it up" and "The stubborn turnip," tug on the string hanging down.

They tried to pull it up (clap, clap). They tried to pull it up (clap, clap).
The stubborn turnip (clap, clap). The stubborn turnip (clap, clap).

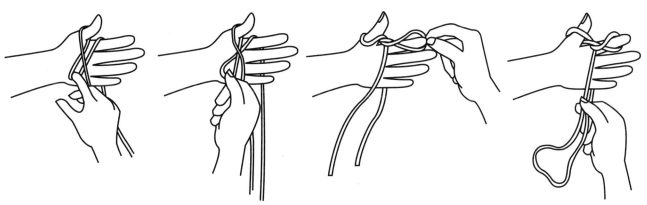

"That's a stubborn turnip," said Pa. He needed help so he called Cow. Cow grabbed Pa. Pa grabbed Ma. Ma grabbed the turnip and they began to pull.

Now, it's a matter of repeating the step. With your right index finger, reach under the front string between the index and middle finger, and pull a loop of the back string to the front under the top string. Give it a clockwise twist and hook the loop around the left middle finger. Point to the corresponding fingers when you say "cow," "pa," and "ma." When you say, "They tried to pull it up" and "The stubborn turnip," tug on the string hanging down.

They tried to pull it up (clap, clap). They tried to pull it up (clap, clap).
The stubborn turnip (clap, clap). The stubborn turnip (clap, clap).

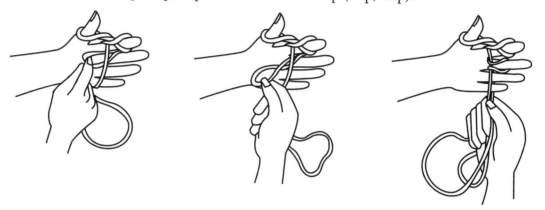

"That's a stubborn turnip," said Cow. She needed help so she called Dog. Dog grabbed Cow. Cow grabbed Pa. Pa grabbed Ma. Ma grabbed the turnip and they began to pull.

Repeat the step. With your right index finger, reach under the front string between the middle and ring finger, and pull a loop of the back string to the front under the top string. Give it a clockwise twist and hook the loop around the left ring finger. Point to the corresponding fingers when you say "dog," "cow," "pa," and "ma." When you say, "They tried to pull it up" and "The stubborn turnip," tug on the string hanging down.

They tried to pull it up (clap, clap). They tried to pull it up (clap, clap).
The stubborn turnip (clap, clap). The stubborn turnip (clap, clap).

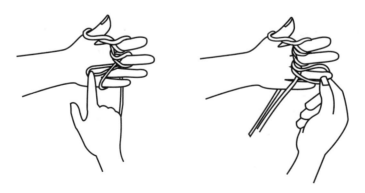

"That's a stubborn turnip," said Dog. He needed help so he called Cat. Cat grabbed Dog. Dog grabbed Cow. Cow grabbed Pa. Pa grabbed Ma. Ma grabbed the turnip and they began to pull.

Repeat the step. With your right index finger, reach under the front string between the ring and pinkie finger, and pull a loop of the back string to the front under the top string. Give it a clockwise twist and hook the loop around the left pinkie finger. Point to the corresponding fingers when you say "cat," "dog," "cow," "pa," and "ma." When you say, "They tried to pull it up" and "The stubborn turnip," tug on the string hanging down.

> They tried to pull it up (clap, clap). They tried to pull it up (clap, clap).
> The stubborn turnip (clap, clap). The stubborn turnip (clap, clap).

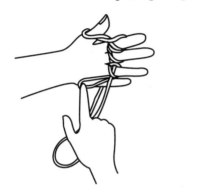 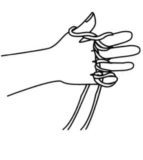 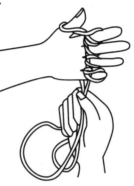

"That's a stubborn turnip," said Cat. No matter how hard they tried, they couldn't pull up the stubborn turnip. They were about to give up when a mouse came by. She said, "Maybe I can help."

With your right hand, grab the dangling string at the bottom and form into a small circle to symbolize a mouse.

"That's a great idea," said Ma Farmer. "Go to the end of the line." So Mouse went to the end of the line. Mouse grabbed Cat. Cat grabbed Dog. Dog grabbed Cow. Cow grabbed Pa. Pa grabbed Ma. Ma grabbed the turnip and they began to pull.

Wiggle the string for the mouse and point to the corresponding fingers when you say "cat," "dog," "cow," "pa," and "ma." When you say, "They tried to pull it up," tug on the string hanging down.

> They tried to pull it up (clap, clap). They tried to pull it up (clap, clap)

And suddenly …

> The turnip came up … a little at first. Then they gave it a giant pull and the stubborn turnip came up!

Release the loop from the thumb.
This is the turnip coming up a little at first.
Then pull the long front string down.
All the loops will release from the fingers.

The turnip was gigantic!

Loop the string around both hands to show a big circle (the giant turnip). Advanced: Form the Cup and Saucer string figure while saying the lines below. 1. Loop strings across both of your palms, behind the pinkies and thumbs. 2. Reach across with your right index finger and pick up the string from the front of the left palm. 3. Pull your hands apart. 4. With the left index finger, repeat steps two and three. 5. Reach over with both thumbs and hook the thumbs under the string on the far side of each index finger. 6. Pull thumbs back to original position. You should have two loops on each thumb. 7. Next, you will "Navajo" the loops. With your mouth, or your other hand, pull the bottom loops over the tops of the other loops on your thumbs. 8. Drop the loops from both pinkies and pull your hands apart. The bowl will be upside down. 9. Tilt your hands so that the bowl is right-side up.

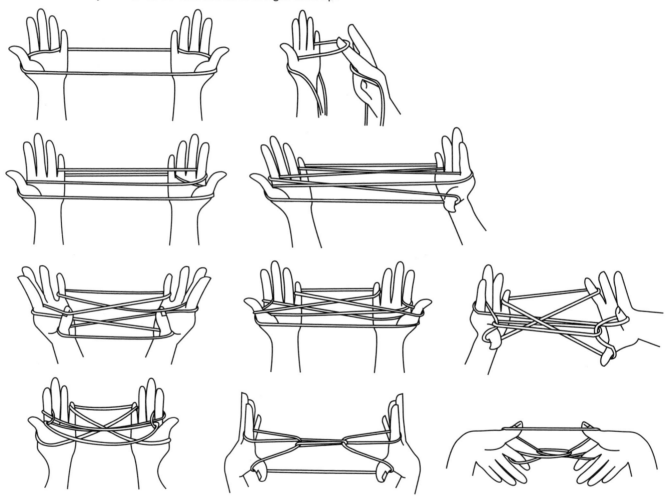

Ma Farmer was so happy that she had enough turnip to make a big bowl of turnip soup for everyone.

Show bowl (Cup and Saucer string figure).

The moral of this story is …

> Never give up (clap, clap). Never give up (clap, clap).
> And you can pull up (clap, clap). The stubborn turnip (clap, clap).

Part II

Draw and Tell

The Emperor's Dragon
A Draw and Tell Inspired by a Chinese Folk Tale

There was once an emperor who lived in the rolling hills of China.

Every day, he loved walking along the rolling hills.

One day during his walk, he saw the most beautiful red flower. The flower reminded him of his favorite animal – the powerful Chinese dragon. The emperor began a search for the artist who could draw him the perfect dragon.

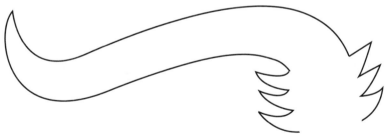

He sailed on the long, windy river.

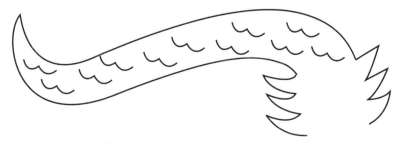

He climbed over tall, towering mountains.

He traveled through the thick, tree-filled forests.

Finally, the emperor came to a place where two villages met.

In those villages were two houses.

In one of those houses lived a young man named Chin. Chin had in his hand a paintbrush.

The emperor cried out, "Are you an artist?"
"Yes," answered Chin, "I am."
The emperor asked, "What do you paint?"
Chin answered, "I paint what my eyes see."

The emperor clapped. "Can you draw a dragon?"
Chin said, "I can try."
With a few strokes of his paintbrush, Chin painted a flaming red crown.

The emperor stared at the painting. It was the perfect Chinese dragon.
Chin was given a place of honor at the palace and dragons covered all of the palace walls.

Catching a Pest
A Drawing Tale in 7 Steps

Kat heard squeaking noises in the house. She said, "Oh no! There's a pest in the house. I must catch it." So first, she searched the floor. [Draw the number 1.]

_____

Then Kat heard noises in the wall. So she followed the sound and found a hole in the wall, near a small crack. [Draw the number 2.]

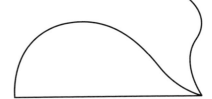

The pest ran out of the hole, from one room to the other. [Draw the number 3.]

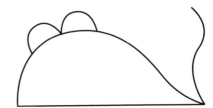

Kat chased it, yelling, "Come back here!" She grabbed a broom. [Draw the number 4.]

Kat ran straight but the pest was quick and turned around. [Draw the number 5.]

Kat finally cornered the pest. It ran around and around but had nowhere to go. [Draw the number 6.]

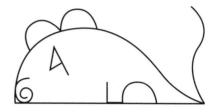

Then Kat scooped up the pest with her dustpan. [Draw first 7.] She quickly swept it out the door. [Draw second 7.]

Kat caught a … MOUSE! [Allow audience to chime in answer when drawing is complete.]

Part III

Cut and Tell

Joseph Had an Overcoat

I first heard this story from my friend and fellow storyteller, John Lehon. This version is adapted from *Joseph Had a Little Overcoat* by Simms Taback.

Take a large piece of pliable poster board and fold it in half lengthwise. Cut out the following pattern. The dotted lines signify where you are to cut. Invite audience to participate when you say, "It got tattered and torn." Practice the cutting so that it flows smoothly with your telling of the story. Timing is crucial in successful delivery of this cut and tell.

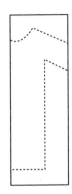

Joseph was a tailor and he made beautiful clothes. One day, he wanted to make something beautiful for himself so he decided to make an overcoat.

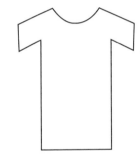

1. Joseph had a warm coat.

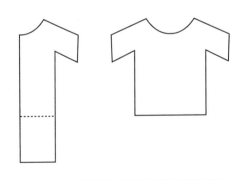

2. But it got tattered and torn. So he made a jacket out of it and wore it to a party.

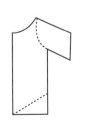

3. Joseph had a snazzy jacket. But it got tattered and torn. So he made a vest out of it and wore it to a reunion.

4. Joseph had a fine vest. But it got tattered and torn. So he made a scarf out of it and wore it to the ice rink.

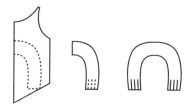

5. Joseph had a soft scarf. But it got tattered and torn. So he made a necktie out of it and wore it to dinner.

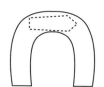

6. Joseph had a handsome necktie. But it got tattered and torn. So he made a handkerchief out of it and used it to wipe his nose when he had the sniffles.

7. Joseph had a useful handkerchief (cough and sniffle into the paper). But it got tattered and torn and … (pause) nasty! So he washed it and made a button out of it and used it to fasten his suspenders.

8. Joseph had a beautiful button. But it got … (Allow audience to respond "tattered and torn" and then shake your head no and say) LOST! Now Joseph had nothing. So Joseph decided to take each piece and make a story out of it. It just goes to show you that you can always make something out of … nothing!

Papa's Teepee
From "The Chief's New Home" by Margie Willis Clary

I first learned this story from my friend and fellow storyteller, Karen Chace. She learned it from Suzette Hawkins, who learned it from the story's creator, Margie Willis Clary. Just like snowflakes, no two stories are exactly alike. A special thank you to Margie Willis Clary for allowing me to share this story with you.

There was once a Native American family. It was winter and the Great Snow was coming. They needed to build a home. So Papa built a strong and sturdy teepee.

1.
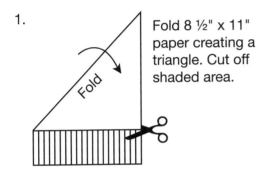
Fold 8 ½" x 11" paper creating a triangle. Cut off shaded area.

2.
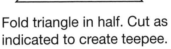
Fold triangle in half. Cut as indicated to create teepee.

3.

Finished teepee.

Mama looked at the teepee and said, "Papa, you built a strong and sturdy teepee but how will we get inside? There is no door."

Papa said, "You are right. I must make a door." So Papa cut a door at the bottom.

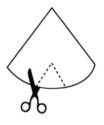
Cut triangular door at the bottom of the teepee.

Mama looked again at the teepee and said, "Papa, you built a strong and sturdy teepee but how will the smoke escape? When it is cold, we will need to build a fire. There is no smoke hole."

Papa said, "You are right. I must make a smoke hole." So Papa cut a hole at the top.

Snip off top of teepee.

Brother looked at the teepee and said, "Papa, you built a strong and sturdy teepee but my dog needs his own door. Can you cut a door for my dog?"

Papa said, "Very well. I will cut a door for your dog." So Papa cut a small door for the Brother's dog.

Cut a smaller triangular door to one side of the big door, on the bottom of the teepee.

Sister looked at the teepee and said, "Papa, you built a strong and sturdy teepee but if brother's dog gets a door, then my cat needs a door too. Can you cut a door for my cat?"

Papa said, "Very well. I will cut a door for your cat." So Papa cut a small door for Sister's cat.

Cut a smaller triangular door to the other side of the big door, on the bottom of the teepee.

Brother looked at the teepee and said, "Papa, you built a strong and sturdy teepee but I need a window to see the night sky. Can you cut a window for me so that I can fall asleep to the twinkling stars?"

Papa said, "Very well. I will cut a window for you." So Papa cut a window for Brother.

Cut a small triangle on one side of the top of the teepee to create a window.

Sister looked at the teepee and said, "Papa, you built a strong and sturdy teepee but I need a window to see the morning sky. Can you cut a window for me so that I can wake up to the rising sun?"

Papa said, "Very well. I will cut a window for you." So Papa cut a window for Sister.

Cut a small triangle on the other side of the top of the teepee to create a window.

Then Papa, Mama, Brother, Sister, Dog, and Cat all settled into their strong and sturdy teepee. They warmed themselves by the fire and the smoke rose through the hole at the top of the teepee. That night, they fell asleep to the twinkling stars. In the morning, they woke up to the rising sun.

When they looked out the window, they couldn't believe their eyes. [Open up teepee and drop to the ground.] The Great Snow had visited overnight. It was a good thing that Papa had built such a strong and sturdy teepee!

The Emperor's New Clothes
Liberally adapted from Hans Christian Anderson's story

Many, many years ago, there was an emperor who loved the finest things in life. But what he fancied most was clothes. He loved clothes made of the finest thread and the silkiest fabric. One day, he decided that he would commission the most exquisite clothes ever made.

Two swindlers heard that the emperor wanted new clothing made. So they devised a scheme. The swindlers said to the emperor, "The clothing we make is so exquisite, only the truly refined will appreciate its quality."

The emperor said, "Splendid. I shall see you tomorrow for a fitting."

The two swindlers went to work and created a pair of pants. The pants were nothing special. They were actually quite ordinary. When the emperor came in, he put on the pair of pants.

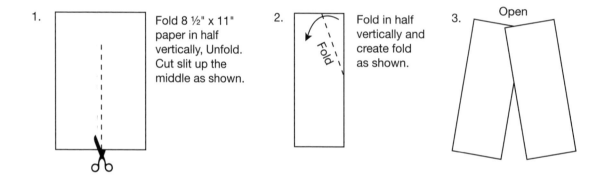

1. Fold 8 ½" x 11" paper in half vertically, Unfold. Cut slit up the middle as shown.

2. Fold in half vertically and create fold as shown.

3. Open

When the emperor asked his advisors what they thought, they all said, "They're perfect!" even though they thought the pants were quite ordinary.

But the two swindlers said, "No, no, no! That will never do. It's not good enough for an emperor like you." They took their scissors and cut off the bottoms, turning them into knickers.

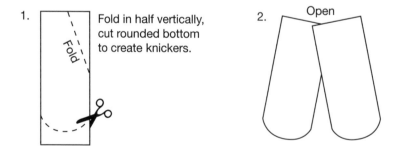

1. Fold in half vertically, cut rounded bottom to create knickers.

2. Open

When the emperor asked his advisors what they thought, they all said, "They're perfect!" even though they thought the knickers were quite ordinary.

But the two swindlers said, "No, no, no! That will never do. It's not good enough for an emperor like you." They took their scissors and cut off more fabric, turning them into Bermuda shorts.

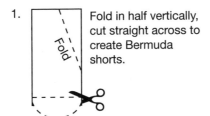 1. Fold in half vertically, cut straight across to create Bermuda shorts.

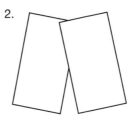 2.

When the emperor asked his advisors what they thought, they all said, "They're perfect!" even though they thought the Bermuda shorts were quite ordinary.

But the two swindlers said, "No, no, no! That will never do. It's not good enough for an emperor like you." They took their scissors and cut off more fabric, turning them into summer shorts.

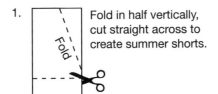 1. Fold in half vertically, cut straight across to create summer shorts.

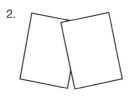 2.

When the emperor asked his advisors what they thought, they all said, "They're perfect!" even though they thought the shorts were quite ordinary.

But the two swindlers said, "No, no, no! That will never do. It's not good enough for an emperor like you." They took their scissors and cut off more fabric, turning them into underwear!

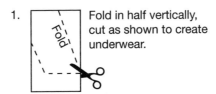 1. Fold in half vertically, cut as shown to create underwear.

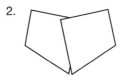 2.

When the emperor asked his advisors what they thought, they all said, "They're perfect!" even though they thought the underwear were quite ridiculous!

The two swindlers smiled and said, "Yes! Yes! Yes! That will do. It's just perfect for an emperor like you."

The emperor called a procession and began parading around town. While all the people of the kingdom thought he looked quite ridiculous, no one dared to say anything to the emperor. They clapped and whistled as he paraded by.

Suddenly a little boy began laughing. He yelled, "Look at the emperor in his underwear!"

Then the whole town began laughing, for it was true. The emperor was in nothing but his royal underwear! Quite embarrassed, he hurried back to his palace and put on a proper pair of pants. The emperor decided he no longer needed the finest clothes. He turned his attentions elsewhere—to his hair.

Snip scissors in the air
when saying the last line.

April Showers
A Fold, Cut and Tell Story

There was once a little girl who loved sitting by the window.

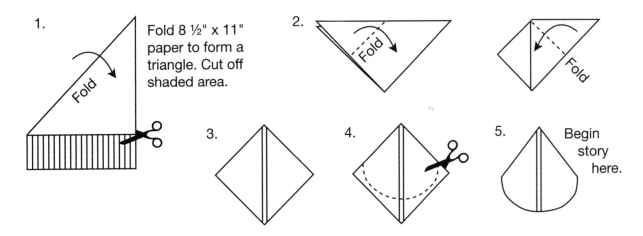

One day, she was sitting by the window, looking out of the curtains.

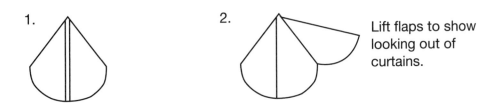

Lift flaps to show looking out of curtains.

Outside, water fell from the sky. She saw tons of tiny little raindrops.

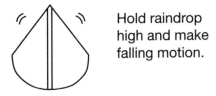

Hold raindrop high and make falling motion.

She wished, more than anything, to go outside and play. But, of course, she couldn't because it was raining. So she began singing.

"Rain, rain, go away
Come again another day
I want to play
Rain, rain, go away."

Continue making falling motion while singing sadly.

But the rain continued to fall.

So the little girl closed her eyes and made a wish. She began singing again.

"April showers
Bring May flowers
April showers
Bring May flowers." Continue making
falling motion
while singing
sadly.

To her surprise, she looked outside and the sun was shining. Then right before her eyes, April showers turned into … May Flowers!

 Open raindrop to
reveal flower.

Big beautiful flowers blossomed. Then a friend came to the window and invited her to play. It was a … ladybug! The little girl's wish came true and she played in the garden all day long.

 Fold flower closed,
back into raindrop
shape. Lift both flaps
to reveal lady bug.
Draw black dots.

The Royal Paper Puzzle

Penelope was a princess of uncommon beauty. She had ruby lips, rosy cheeks, and a cute curls that framed her pretty face.

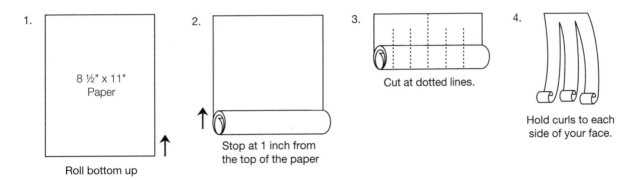

1. 8 ½" x 11" Paper

Roll bottom up

2. Stop at 1 inch from the top of the paper

3. Cut at dotted lines.

4. Hold curls to each side of your face.

Princess Penelope was of the marrying age. The king wanted her to find a husband but she said that no ordinary man would do. A man with brawn was not enough. Penelope wanted a husband with a brain.

Upon her father's urging, she devised a puzzle. Penelope would marry the man who could solve the puzzle.

The King sent out a proclamation, "Hear ye! Hear ye! Any man who solves Princess Penelope's Paper Puzzle shall win her hand in marriage."

Men from within the kingdom and beyond the kingdom lined up for a chance to win the princess's hand. Not only was she beautiful, she was also rich!!

When everyone was gathered in the courtyard, Princess Penelope said, "The man who solves this puzzle shall win my heart. Here is the task. Cut this small piece of square paper so that I can walk through it. No piece of paper must be wasted."

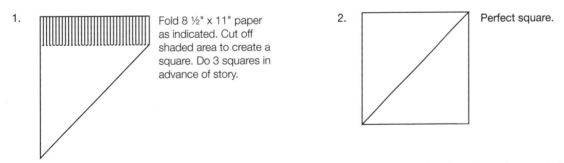

1. Fold 8 ½" x 11" paper as indicated. Cut off shaded area to create a square. Do 3 squares in advance of story.

2. Perfect square.

The men laughed. Some of them thought, "No one will marry the princess, for that is an impossible task." Some of them thought, "That is easy! I can do that!" Those that thought they could solve the puzzle stood in line. For hours, Princess Penelope watched as the men cut and cut but did not make the cut.

Cut strips of paper and let fall to ground.

From *Handmade Tales: Stories to Make and Take* by Dianne de Las Casas. Westport, CT: Libraries Unlimited. Copyright © 2008.

One day grew into two and then into three. Word of the impossibility of the royal paper puzzle spread. Noble men, dukes, and princes came from far and wide.

One conceited duke rode into the courtyard on a tall horse. He exclaimed, "Princess Penelope! I am a cut above the rest. Let me show these fools how it is done."

Penelope smiled and said, "Of course. All you have to do is cut this small piece of square paper so that I can walk through it. No piece of paper must be wasted." She handed him the square of paper and scissors and he began cutting in earnest.

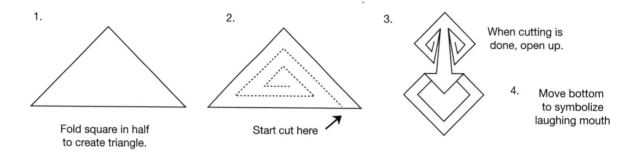

"I have it!" he cried out! But when he held up his paper, the entire courtyard laughed. It was a disaster. The duke lowered his head in shame and rode away.

Next, a pampered prince rode into the courtyard in a carriage. He exclaimed, "Princess Penelope! These men just don't cut it. Let me show them how it is done."

Penelope smiled and said, "Of course. All you have to do is cut this small piece of square paper so that I can walk through it. No piece of paper must be wasted." She handed him the square of paper and scissors and he began cutting in earnest.

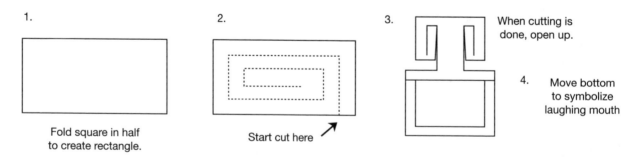

"It's done!" he cried out! But when the prince held up his paper, the entire courtyard laughed. His creation was a disaster, just like all the others. The prince stormed out in his carriage.

All the while, a handsome but poor young man named Patrick watched carefully as each man tried and failed to solve Princess Penelope's paper puzzle. He stepped forward and said, "With your kind permission, I would like to try, Your Majesty."

The King looked at Patrick in his poor, patched clothing and said, "You?! Ha! My daughter cannot marry such a ragamuffin. Besides, you will fail just like the others. Save yourself the humiliation and go home."

"Please, sir, I beg for a chance," said Patrick politely.

Penelope smiled and said, "The proclamation does say 'Any man.'" She handed him the square of paper and scissors. "All you have to do is cut this small piece of square paper so that I can walk through it. No piece of paper must be wasted."

Patrick nodded and went to work. He snipped and snipped and in just a few short cuts, he was finished. "I'm done, Princess." He opened the paper to the gasps and amazement of the crowd.

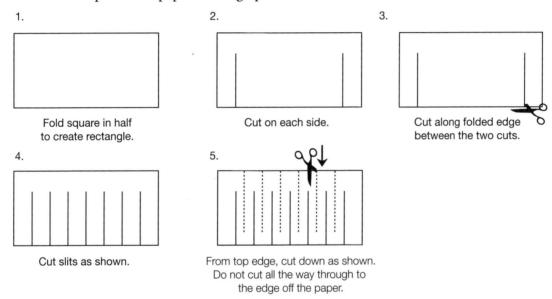

1. Fold square in half to create rectangle.

2. Cut on each side.

3. Cut along folded edge between the two cuts.

4. Cut slits as shown.

5. From top edge, cut down as shown. Do not cut all the way through to the edge off the paper.

"You did it!" Princess Penelope exclaimed. "You cut the paper so that I can walk through it."

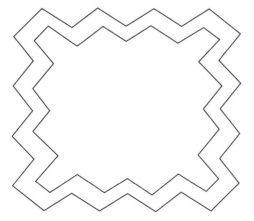

And Princess Penelope did just that. She walked through the paper and gave Patrick a peck on the cheek. He blushed and smiled.

Princess Penelope and Patrick were married. Since they both had a passion for paper, they opened a store called "Pat and Penny's Paper Puzzles." It was positively perfect.

The Pilot's Wheel

One day, Jack was bored, sitting in his room. [Start with a square of paper.]

1.
8 ½"

11"

2.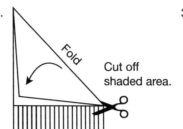
Fold
Cut off
shaded area.

3.

He stared out the window and wished he could do something fun. [Fold the square in half from left to right. Then fold the paper in half from bottom to top.]

1.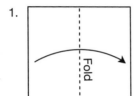
Fold

2.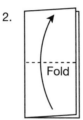
Fold

3.

So he decided to leave the house in search of something to do. Jack ran around the corner. [Fold the bottom right-hand corner to meet the top left-hand corner, forming a triangle.]

1.
Fold

2.

He ran around another corner. [Fold the top left-hand corner of the triangle over so that the left edge is now even with the opposite sloping side. It will form another triangle.]

1.
Fold

2.

He "cut" across a neighbor's yard. [Cut out the figure as shown.]

1.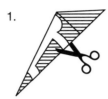

2.

He walked until he came to the river where he saw a steamboat anchored on the other side. [Rotate the paper upside down to create an anchor. Then rotate the figure right-side up to create a person.] This is Jack.

1.

2.

Jack crossed the bridge and boarded the steamboat. [Show Jack "moving." Then open half of the figure to reveal a "bridge."]

The captain said, "Hello, young lad! Are you interested in piloting this ship's wheel?" [Open the rest of the figure to reveal a pilot's wheel.]

Jack was so excited! For on that day, Jack became "Captain Jack," steering the steamboat down the great Mississippi river! [Salute your audience and "steer" the pilot's wheel.]

The King's Advisor

For this story, you will need scissors and three 8 ½ × 11" sheets of paper. When the story is finished, you can teach your audience how to make their own six-page books. Then the budding authors can write and illustrate their own mini-storybooks.

There was once a king who needed an advisor. He wanted an advisor who was clever and kind. So the king devised a puzzle and made an announcement.

"Hear ye, hear ye! I am seeking a new advisor. The person who can create a six-page book about of one sheet of paper without cutting the paper apart shall win. He will become my advisor and win a treasure chest full of gold."

Hold up an 8 ½ × 11" sheet of paper.

A dastardly duke stepped forward and said, "I am perfect for the job. Hand me the paper."

(He wasn't even polite enough to say please.) The King handed the duke the sheet of paper and the duke began folding. When he was finished, he said, "Ta da!"

Fold the sheet of paper into fourths. First, fold the top to the bottom. Then fold the left side to meet with the right side.

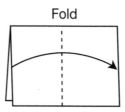
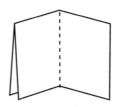

The king examined the book carefully. He opened it up and announced, "This book has only two pages. Is there anyone else who would like to try?"

A narcissistic nobleman stepped forward and said, "I am perfect for the job. Hand me the paper."

(He wasn't even polite enough to say please.) The King handed the nobleman the sheet of paper and the nobleman began folding and then made a cut. When he was finished, he said, "Voila!"

Fold a sheet of paper into eighths. First, fold the top to the bottom. Then fold the left to meet with the right side. Then again, fold the top to the bottom. Open the paper up. It should have eight sections. Again, fold the top to the bottom. Next, cut a slit halfway down the middle.

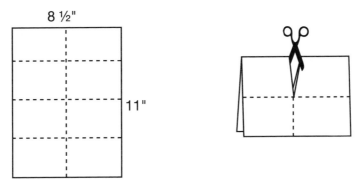

Fold the paper in half from left to right. Then fold the first flap at the top halfway down. Give the paper a quarter turn to the right and you have a four page book.

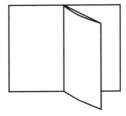

The king examined the book carefully. He opened it up and announced, "This book has only four pages. Is there anyone else who would like to try?"

A shy shepherd stepped forward and said, "I may not be perfect for the job but I would like to try. May I please have the paper?"

(Finally! Someone with manners!) The King said, "With pleasure," and handed the shepherd the sheet of paper. The shepherd began folding and then made a cut. When he was finished, he said, "At your service, your majesty." He took a deep bow and handed the king his book.

This book is nearly the same as the one above except that it is folded differently. Fold a sheet of paper into eighths. First, fold the top to the bottom. Then fold the left to meet with the right side. Then again, fold the top to the bottom. Open the paper up. It should have eight sections. Again, fold the top to the bottom. Next, cut a slit halfway down the middle.

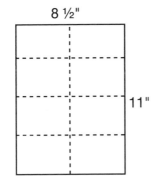

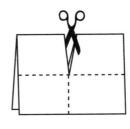

Turn the paper so that it is horizontal. Fold the paper in half from top to bottom. Then take the two sides and push the paper together until it forms an "X." Fold the book closed. It will have six pages inside.

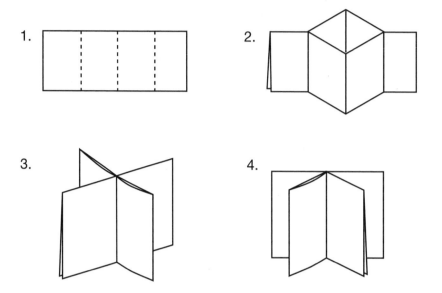

The king examined the book carefully. He opened it up and announced, "This book has six pages. You have won the contest, young shepherd! You are my new advisor and you win a treasure chest full of gold."

The shepherd smiled. "Thank you, your highness. My first order of business will be to use the gold to build a library full of books. Knowledge is the most valuable treasure there is."

The king was delighted. "An excellent idea!" The king knew that he had indeed chosen wisely. The shepherd was clever and kind. From then on, the kingdom flourished, both from good leadership as well as good books.

Hold up all the books made during this story.

The Magic Star

This story is so much fun and perfect for a unit on space or solar systems.

1. Though I want to take a peek

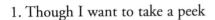
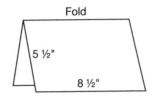

Fold 8 ½" x 11" paper in half. Peek from behind folded paper.

2. During the day, I play hide and seek

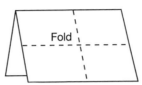

Fold in half vertically and horizontally to form a crease. Unfold.

3. My cousin, the Sun, shines so bright

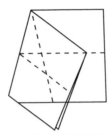

Fold from the vertical crease to meet center line.

4. But I prefer to come out at night

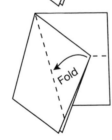

Bring the corner left so that the edges meet. Fold.

5. My friends and I twinkle from afar

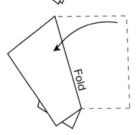

Bring the left corner around

6. Can you guess just what we are?

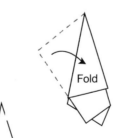

Bring second corner right until the edges meet. Fold.

7. In case you didn't know, I'm a ... Star!

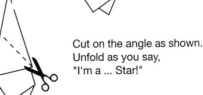

Cut on the angle as shown. Unfold as you say, "I'm a ... Star!"

Part IV

Paper Tales (Fold and Tell, Scroll Books, and Other Paper Tales)

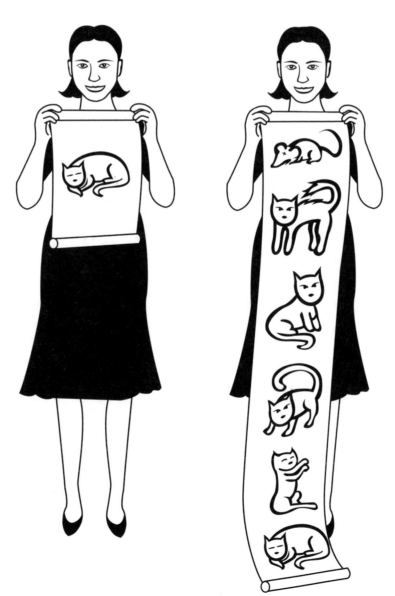

Grandma's Party
A Matryoshka Story

The concept of this story is based on Russian Nesting Dolls known as Matryoshka. A smaller doll nests inside a bigger doll to form a set of five dolls. These dolls are made using a note-folding technique that I adapted, which I learned in elementary school!

To begin this story, the paper cutting and folding must be done ahead of time. Grandma is the biggest doll and each of the dolls nests inside her. To create the small dolls, use the same pattern but trim 1" of paper from each side, vertically and horizontally. Each successive doll will be smaller than the last. Decorate the dolls with geometric patterns, keeping the shapes simple. I used a Russian nesting doll as my inspiration to draw the face. Colored pencils, crayons, and even markers work well to color the dolls.

To hold all the dolls when they are not in use, I created a house out of a vertical 6" × 9" envelope with a brad closure. I snipped off the sides of the top to create a roofline and decorated the house. I made the door by tracing the size of the largest nesting doll.

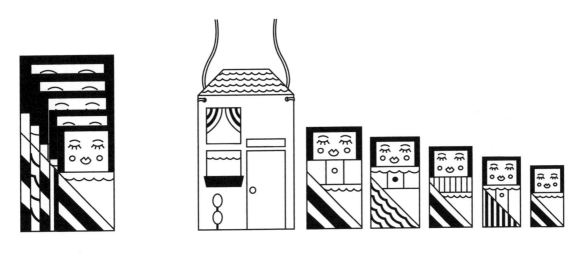

Folding the Doll

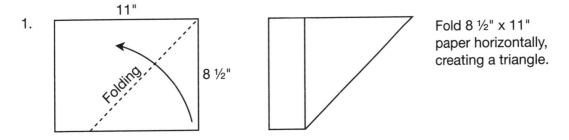

1. 11" / 8 ½" / Folding

Fold 8 ½" x 11" paper horizontally, creating a triangle.

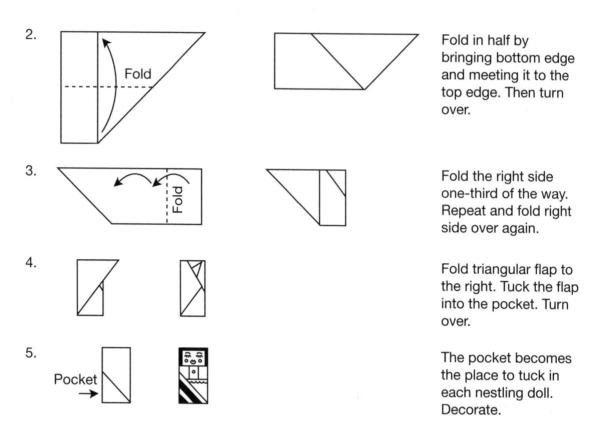

2. Fold in half by bringing bottom edge and meeting it to the top edge. Then turn over.

3. Fold the right side one-third of the way. Repeat and fold right side over again.

4. Fold triangular flap to the right. Tuck the flap into the pocket. Turn over.

5. The pocket becomes the place to tuck in each nestling doll. Decorate.

Baby lived with Little Sister, Big Sister, Mama, and Grandma. [Pull out each doll from their nesting positions.]

One day, Baby disappeared. [Hide Baby away.] Little Sister said, "Oh no! Baby is gone. I must find her." So Little Sister left to find Baby. [Hide Little Sister away.]

Little Sister and Baby were gone for a long time. Big Sister said, "Oh no! Little Sister and Baby are gone. I must find them!" So Big Sister left to find Little Sister and Baby. [Hide Big Sister away.]

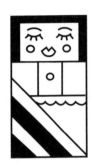

Big Sister, Little Sister, and Baby were gone for a long time. Mama said, "Oh no! Big Sister, Little Sister, and Baby are gone. I must find them!" So Mama left to find Big Sister, Little Sister, and Baby. [Hide Mama away.]

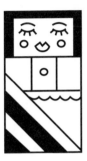

Now Grandma was all alone. She said, "Where did everyone go?"

Grandma called out, "Where is everyone?" She looked everywhere but could not find Mama, Big Sister, Little Sister, and Baby. [Move Grandma around as if looking for her family.]

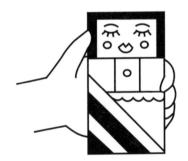

Then Grandma left the house. As soon as she stepped outside, Mama, Big Sister, Little Sister, and Baby yelled, "SURPRISE!"

It was Grandma's birthday and they had a surprise party for her. Woo hoo! [Hold Grandma in one hand and the other dolls in the other hand. Dance them around as if they are having a party.] When the party was finished, it was time to go home. Little Sister picked up Baby. [Tuck Baby into Little Sister.] Big Sister picked up Little Sister. [Tuck Little Sister into Big Sister.] Mama picked up Big Sister. [Tuck Big Sister into Mama.] And Grandma carried everyone home. [Tuck Mama and everyone into Grandma.] They all had such a big day that when they got home, they all went to sleep. [Turn nesting dolls flat and make snoring sounds.]

The Boy Who Drew Cats
Japan

This is one of my favorite stories from Japan. The scroll story method works well for "The Boy Who Drew Cats." To create the scroll, you will need two empty paper towel tubes, eight feet of poster paper, double-stick tape, and black paint. Cut the poster paper to the width of the paper towel tubes. Double stick each end of the poster paper to the tubes, being sure to completely cover the tube. Stretch out the roll on a flat surface. It helps to weight down each end to prevent rolling. Using the vertical orientation of the scroll, paint a series of cats in different positions, placing adequate space between each illustration. The rat should be the last illustration at the top of the scroll.

When you tell the story, one or two cats are revealed as you unroll the scroll from the bottom up. The rat is the last illustration to be revealed.

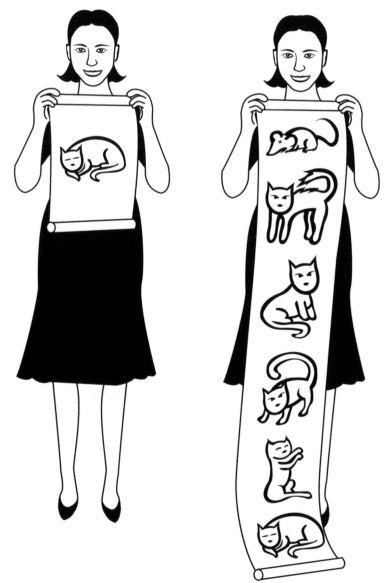

A long time ago in Japan, there lived a poor farmer and his wife. Their youngest son did not have the heart of a farmer. He had the heart of an artist. He spent all of his time drawing cats!

Big cats, small cats, short cats, tall cats.
Here cats, there cats. Everywhere, cats!
Cats, cats, cats. He drew cats, cats, cats.

Unroll scroll and reveal two cats as you say the refrain.

His father said, "Son, since you cannot farm, you must go to the village temple and study to become a priest."

The boy was taken to the temple to study for the priesthood. An old priest became his teacher and the boy learned quickly. But the boy did not have the heart of a priest. He had the heart of an artist. When he needed to spend his time studying, he did not. He spent all of his time drawing cats.

Big cats, small cats, short cats, tall cats.
Here cats, there cats. Everywhere, cats!
Cats, cats, cats. He drew cats, cats, cats.

Unroll scroll and reveal the next two cats as you say the refrain.

The old priest called the boy and said, "Son, since you are unable to study for the priesthood, I must send you away. But here is some advice. Avoid large places. Stick to small spaces."

The boy left the temple with his pack on his back. He walked for some time and needed shelter. In the distance, he saw a temple. He knocked and found that the temple was empty. When he went inside, he discovered white floors and white walls. His heart jumped with joy as pulled out his paint and brushes. He spent all night drawing cats.

Big cats, small cats, short cats, tall cats.
Here cats, there cats. Everywhere, cats!
Cats, cats, cats. He drew cats, cats, cats.

Unroll scroll and reveal the last cat as you say the refrain.

When he was finished, he was tired and needed to sleep. As he searched for a place to sleep, he remembered the old priest's words. "Avoid large places. Stick to small spaces."

So the boy found a small cabinet with a sliding door and climbed inside. As he dozed off, he heard strange noises. Hissing and howling. Grunting and growling. The boy was frightened and stayed in the small cabinet.

When daylight came, the sounds stopped. He climbed out of the cabinet and saw a huge goblin rat lying lifeless on the floor.

Unroll scroll and reveal the rat.

The boy knew immediately that his cats had come to life during the night and saved his life. The boy bowed and said, "Thank you, honorable cats!"

From that time forward, the boy with the heart of an artist drew to his heart's content. And, of course, he spent all of his time drawing cats!

Big cats, small cats, short cats, tall cats.
Here cats, there cats. Everywhere, cats!
Cats, cats, cats. He drew cats, cats, cats.

He became a famous artist known all over Japan for his beautiful drawings of … cats!

Roll the scroll back up as you chant the refrain for the last time. Leave the first cat revealed as you say, "beautiful drawings of … cats." Point to the illustration when you say, "cats."

The Girl Who Used Her Wits
China

There was once a family with a father, his three sons, and his two daughters-in-law. The two daughters-in-law had just married the two oldest sons.

They soon grew homesick and they pestered their father-in-law to grant permission to visit their mother. The old man said, "You may leave only if each of you brings me fire wrapped in paper and wind wrapped in paper. If you fulfill your tasks, you may leave as often as you wish. If you fail, you may never return here."

The two girls hastily agreed and chattered happily as they traveled home to their mother's house. Suddenly, they realized their folly. It was an impossible task! Who could wrap wind or fire in paper?! They sat down by the side of the road and began to cry.

Just then, a young peasant girl was riding by on her horse. She stopped and asked, "Why are you crying?"

The two noble wives told her the whole story and the peasant girl said, "That is not so bad. There is a simple solution. Come with me."

The peasant girl brought the two noble wives to her house. She made a paper lantern and handed it to the first wife. "This is fire wrapped in paper."

1.
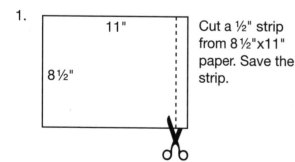
Cut a ½" strip from 8 ½"x11" paper. Save the strip.

2.
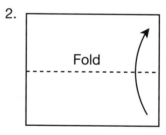
Fold paper in half horizontally. Fold should be at the bottom.

3.
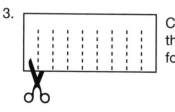
Cut 1" slits across the length of the folded sheet.

4.
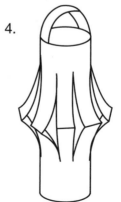
Open paper and join ends together in a circle, with the folds pointing outward. Secure bottom and top with tape. Tape handle to the top. The paper lantern is complete.

Then the peasant girl created a beautiful fan. She handed the paper fan to the second wife. "This is wind wrapped in paper."

1.
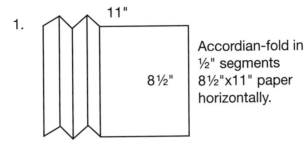
Accordian-fold in ½" segments 8½"x11" paper horizontally.

2.
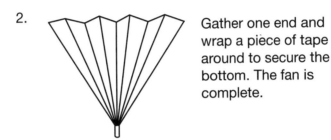
Gather one end and wrap a piece of tape around to secure the bottom. The fan is complete.

The two wives thanked the young girls and dashed home, excited that their solution was so simple. When they showed the old man their objects, he said, "I have been outwitted! Who did this?"

The two wives told him about the young peasant girl. The old man said, "If that girl is so wise, then she needs to marry my youngest son."

So the girl who used her wits married the noble man's youngest son. The old man was so impressed by her wisdom that he made her the head of the house.

The Magic Story Starter

This is a popular children's game that I played as a child and that my children love to play. I knew it as the "cootie catcher." Nowadays, it is called a fortune teller. I have adapted the fortune teller and turned it into a "Magic Story Starter." This is a great exercise for children (and adults!) to use their imaginations and practice their storytelling skills. It may seem a little complex at first but once you make your first one, you will easily master folding and using a story starter.

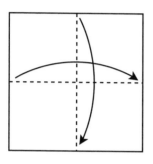

Start with a square of paper. Fold each side in half, creating a crease down the middle, both vertically and horizontally.

Fold each corner in to meet in the middle.

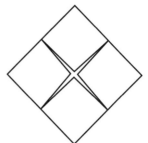

Turn the paper over. Fold in each corner to meet in the middle. Turn the paper over again. On each square, write a story opening.

Story Openings:
Once upon a time …
Long, long ago …
In a land far away …
In the good old days

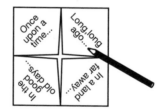

Turn the paper over again. In each one of the triangles, write numbers 1 through 8 at the top. Here, a main story character is introduced. There are eight triangles.

1. There lived a little girl …
2. There was once a terrible ogre …
3. There was an old woman …
4. There was a little boy …
5. There lived a wolf …
6. There was once a woodcutter …
7. There lived a mean old man …
8. There was a huge giant …

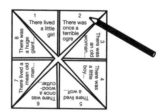

Open all the flaps to reveal more triangles. Under each flap, write an action that corresponds with the character on flap above. You do not need to write numbers inside.

1. Who flew on a magic carpet and landed …
2. Who traveled to the lands of trolls to …
3. Who found a magic stick and …
4. Who found a diamond and …
5. Who found a talking stone. It said …
6. Who fell into a hole and …
7. Who was captured by maniac monkeys and …
8. Who was caught by a witch and …

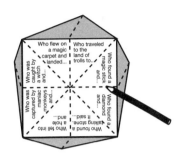

Now you will need to configure the story starter. Close the flaps and turn the story starter over so that you see the story openings. Place your thumb under one flap and your index finger under another flap. Bring the two points together to meet in the middle. Do the same with the other side. It will look like a four-petal flower.

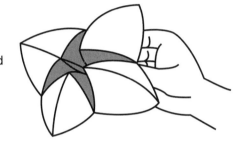

How the story starter works:

1. Each side opens like a puppet's mouth. Begin by asking someone to choose a story opening. Say each word out loud and flap the story starter open from side to side. One flap per word.

2. Ask the person to choose a number. Flap the story starter open from side to side however many times the number indicates. For example, if a person chooses 4, you will flap the story starter four times.

3. Repeat the above step. Ask the person to choose a number. Flap the story starter open from side to side however many times the number indicates. For example, if a person chooses 3, you will flap the story starter three times. (Even numbers will bring you to the same set of characters. Odd numbers will bring you to a different set of characters.)

4. Ask the person to choose a number one last time. This time, you will read what is under the number. (For example, if someone chose 2, you would read, "There was terrible ogre …") Then lift the flap and read what is underneath. ("Who traveled to the land of trolls to …")

5. The person would continue the story. This makes a great storytelling and story writing exercise. If you use this with students, they can create their own magic story starters.

6. When in doubt about how to use a story starter (fortune teller), ask an upper elementary student. He or she will know!

The Great Pirate Adventure

For this story, you will need one large sheet of newspaper, a pair of scissors, and tape. I purposely kept this story simple by using only one piece of newspaper. When I tell this story, I give Captain Snaggletooth a low, growly pirate's voice. Boys, especially, love Captain Snaggletooth.

Christopher lived in a house by the beach.

1.

Large sheet of newspaper

2.

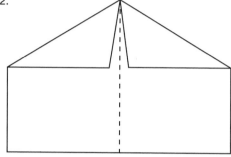

Fold top of each side to the middle of the page, to form two triangles.

Each day, he loved looking out of the window. More than anything, he longed to have a great pirate adventure. He wanted to board a pirate ship and become a … pirate!

1.

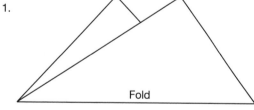

Fold bottom of paper up to form two triangular points.

2.

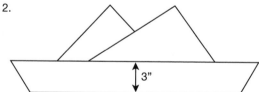

Fold bottom up again about 3" to form the ship's hull. Show this side to the audience.

One day, he looked out of the window and saw a big ship. It was a … pirate's ship!

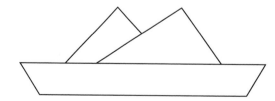

So Christopher snuck out of the house and boarded the ship. He played on the ship for a while and didn't notice that the ship began to sail.

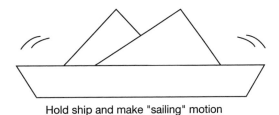

Hold ship and make "sailing" motion

Christopher was stuck! The ship was commanded by a fierce pirate named Captain Snaggletooth. Captain Snaggletooth was looking out of his telescope when he spotted Christopher on the deck.

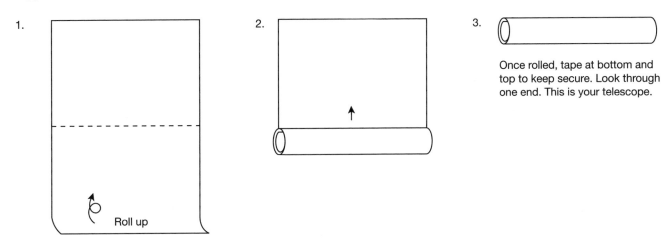

Once rolled, tape at bottom and top to keep secure. Look through one end. This is your telescope.

Roll up

"Ahoy, there, matey! What do ye be doing on me ship?"

Christopher stammered, "I, I just wanted to be a pirate."

Captain Snaggletooth said, "But you're not a pirate. You're a stowaway! I should make ye walk the plank but today is your lucky day because I need a deckhand. You're going to spend your time swabbing the deck!"

Poor Christopher was given a mop. Every day, he swabbed the deck.

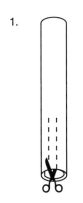

Cut slits all the way around the bottom of the tube, about one-third of the way up the tube. Swish "broom" from side to side to create the motion swabbing the deck.

One day, Captain Snaggletooth said, "We've been out to sea too long. The first matey to spy land will receive a chest of treasure!"

Christopher longed to go home so every day, he looked to the horizon, checking for land. One day, he picked up Captain Snaggletooth's telescope and looked through. In the distance, he saw a tall tree!

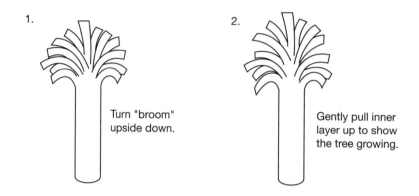

1. Turn "broom" upside down.

2. Gently pull inner layer up to show the tree growing.

Christopher called out, "Land, ho!"

Captain Snaggletooth was pleased. He said, "Matey, since ye spotted the land, I am going to promote you from deckhand to pirate! And, you get a chest full of treasure to boot!"

Christopher the Pirate said, "Thank you, Captain, but all I really want is to go home."

So Christopher returned home. From that time on, when he wanted a big adventure, he no longer stowed away on pirate's ship. Instead, he stayed in his backyard and climbed into his tree house.

Gary's Wings

For this story, you will need a U.S. one dollar bill. As a child, I remember learning how to fold dollar bills into rings and wings. That is where the inspiration for this story came from. This would be a great story to share if a child is accompanying you on a flight.

Gary and his mother were flying to visit his grandparents in another state. Flying made Gary nervous so his mom brought him to see the pilot.

In the cockpit, the pilot smiled. He said, "I used to be nervous when I first started flying. But then I looked out of the window and saw all the beautiful sights. I felt like a bird. Look below. You can see the mountains."

Start with the dollar bill face down. Fold the bottom corners of the bill up so that the left and right sides are even with the top edge of the bill. Flip the bill so that the audience can see the face (it will be upside down). This is your mountain.

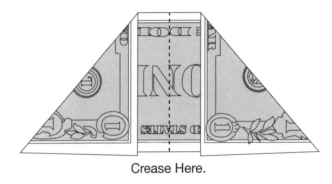

Crease Here.

"Cool!" said Gary. "I've never seen mountains like this before."

Then the pilot pointed out the window again. "Now, we're flying over water. Look at the ships."

Gary looked out of the window and, sure enough, he saw a big boat. "Wow!"

Make a crease down the center of the figure. Next, fold the bottom edge up so that it just covers the "N." It will look like a boat. Show the side that says, "THE UNITED STATES OF AMERICA" to the audience.

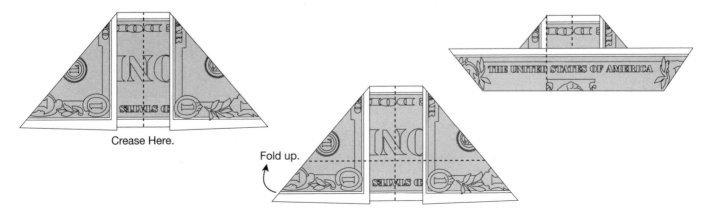

Crease Here.

Fold up.

Gary said, "I don't feel so nervous anymore. I feel like a bird too."

The pilot smiled. "That's great! Now I am making you an honorary pilot."

To make the wings, fold the right side over to the left as shown in the illustration. Then fold it back along the center line of the bill.

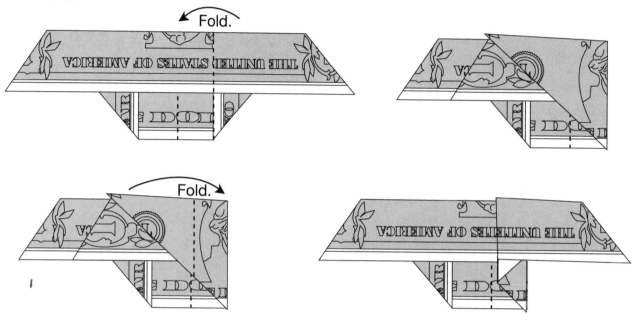

Repeat the step with the other side. Fold the left side over to the right as shown in the illustration. Then fold it back along the center line of the bill.

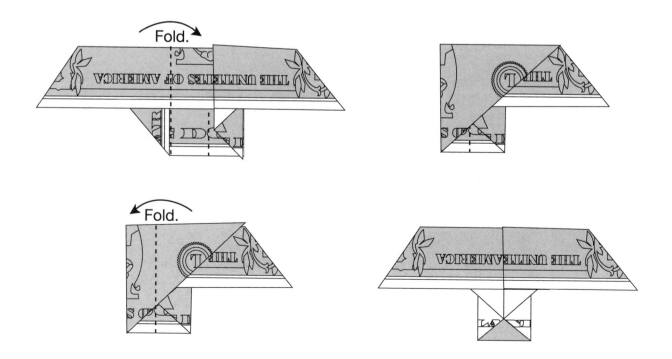

Here's the final step. Fold the bottom corners up to make a point Turn the wings over and show the audience.

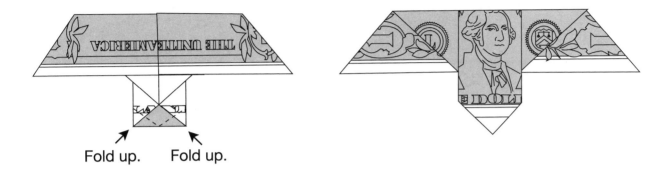

Fold up.   Fold up.

The pilot smiled at Gary and said, "Here are your pilot's wings."

When Gary went back to his seat, he proudly wore his pilot's wings over his heart.

Hold wings over your heart.

Part V

Hand Stories

Mr. Wiggle and Mr. Waggle

This is a great hand story for the very young. I also find that older children like to learn this story (with the pretext that they will use it with younger children).

This is Mr. Wiggle [make thumbs up sign with right hand and wiggle thumb in the air].

This is Mr. Waggle [make thumbs up sign with left hand and wiggle thumb in the air].

Let's put them inside their houses. Open the door [open fists, extending four fingers].

Put them inside [lay thumbs against palms].

Close the door [close four fingers over the thumbs].

Mr. Wiggle lived in a house on top of a hill over here [shake closed right fist].

And Mr. Waggle lived in a house on top of a hill over there [shake closed left fist].

One day, Mr. Wiggle [shake closed right fist].

decided to visit Mr. Waggle [shake closed left fist].

So he opened the door [open fist, extending four fingers].

He came outside [lift thumb up].

And he closed the door [close four fingers over palm].

Then he traveled up the hill and down the hill and up the hill and down the hill and up the hill and down the hill [up and down motions with hand as if traveling over a hill towards other closed fist]

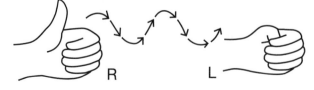

until he was at Mr. Waggle's house [hand should arrive at closed fist].

Mr. Wiggle knocked on the door [with right hand, knock on closed left fist].

Knock, knock, knock
But there was no answer

So he traveled down the hill and up the hill and down the hill and up the hill and down the hill and up the hill [up and down motions with hand as if traveling over a hill towards other hill home] until he was home.

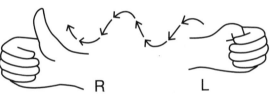

He opened the door [extend four fingers].

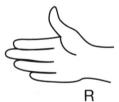

He went inside [fold thumb down].

And he closed the door [close four fingers over the thumb].

The very next day
Mr. Waggle [shake closed left fist]

decided to visit Mr. Wiggle [shake closed right fist].

So he opened the door [open fist, extending four fingers].

He came outside [lift thumb up].

And he closed the door [close four fingers over palm].

Then he traveled up the hill and down the hill and up the hill and down the hill and up the hill and down the hill [up and down motions with hand as if traveling over a hill towards other closed fist]

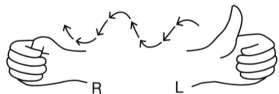

until he was at Mr. Wiggle's house [hand should arrive at closed fist].

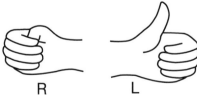

Mr. Waggle knocked on the door [with right hand, knock on closed left fist].

Knock, knock, knock.
But there was no answer

So he traveled down the hill and up the hill and down the hill and up the hill and down the hill and up the hill [up and down motions with hand as if traveling over a hill towards other hill home]
until he was home.

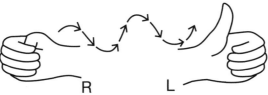

He opened the door [extend four fingers].

He went inside [fold thumb down].

And he closed the door [close four fingers over the thumb].

The very next day,
Mr. Wiggle [shake closed right hand]

and Mr. Waggle [shake closed left hand].

Decided to visit each other.
So they traveled up the hill and down the hill and up the hill and down the hill and up the hill [up and down motions with both hands as if traveling towards each other]
until they met each other.

"Hello Mr. Waggle," said Mr. Wiggle [move right thumb up and down as if talking].

"Hello Mr. Wiggle," replied Mr. Waggle [move left thumb up and down as if talking].

"How are you?" asked Mr. Wiggle [move right thumb up and down as if talking].

"I'm fine, how are you?" replied Mr. Waggle [move left thumb up and down as if talking].

They had a nice, long conversation [move both thumbs up and down]

until the sun began to set and it was time to go home.

So they gave each other a big hug [wrap thumbs around each other twice].

They waved goodbye [wiggle both thumbs to wave goodbye].

And they traveled down the hill and up the hill and down the hill and up the hill and down the hill and up the hill [up and down motions with hand as if traveling over a hill towards other hill home] until they were home.

They opened their doors [extend four fingers on each hand].

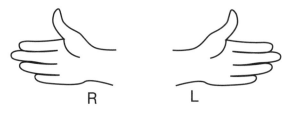

They went inside [fold both thumbs down].

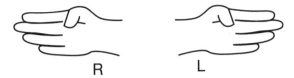

And they closed their doors [close four fingers on each hand over the thumbs].

When the moon rose high in the sky, Mr. Wiggle and Mr. Waggle fell fast asleep [put two hands together and placed on one side of your tilted head to make sleeping motion (you could also add snoring sounds, an optional but very funny ending)].

The Wide Mouth Frog

A tale from North America, the most charming version of this story was taught to me by storyteller and musician Dan Keding. Dan used both of his hands to form the head of the frog, much to the delight of his audience. I found that forming the frog took some practice, but it is well worth it. Each time the frog speaks, create the frog with your hands. Exaggerate the dialogue of the frog, making him loud as well as wide. I have added more hand motions to portray the other characters in the story. Once you learn this story, you'll never forget the "props" for your story because they are always with you!

1.

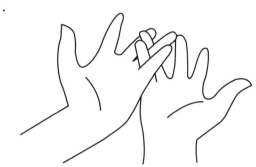

2.

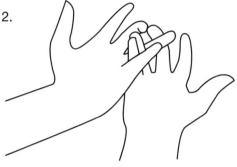

3.

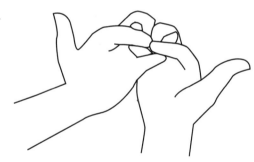

4.

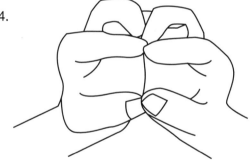

The Wide Mouth Frog lived in a pond. [Form frog with your hands.] One day, he decided to venture out to see the wide, wide world.

As he hopped along, he came upon a red animal flapping her wings. [Extend arms out and flap.]

[Form frog.] The Wide Mouth Frog said, "HELLO! Who are you and what do you eat?"

The animal [flap arms] said, "I am a … [Pause slightly to allow audience to chime in answer] bird. And I eat wet, wiggly worms. [Make a wiggly worm by moving index finger back and forth.]

[Form frog.] The Wide Mouth Frog said, "OH! That's nice." And he hopped on.

As he hopped along, he came upon a black and white animal swishing her tail back and forth.
[Wave backside from side to side. This will get a laugh from the audience.]

[Form frog.] The Wide Mouth Frog said, "HELLO! Who are you and what do you eat?"

The animal [swish tail] said, "Moooooo. I am a … [Pause slightly to allow audience to chime in answer] cow. And I eat great, green grass. [Make grass by moving both hands back and forth.]

[Form frog.] The Wide Mouth Frog said, "OH! That's nice." And he hopped on.

As he hopped along, he came upon a tall, furry brown animal with big claws and sharp teeth.
[Hold up both hands and bend fingers to make claws. Scrunch up face to look mean.]

[Form frog.] The Wide Mouth Frog said, "HELLO! Who are you and what do you eat?"

The animal [snarl and make clawing motion] said, "Grrrrrrrrowl. I am a … [Pause slightly to allow audience to chime in answer] bear. And I eat sweet, sticky honey.
[Wipe chin with both hands and make slurping sounds.]

[Form frog.] The Wide Mouth Frog said, "OH! That's nice." And he hopped on.

As he hopped along, he came upon a long green animal with a big jaw and sharp teeth.
[Elongate arms and put hands together, opening and closing hands to make snapping sounds.]

[Form frog.] The Wide Mouth Frog said, "HELLO! Who are you and what do you eat?"

The animal [clap hands together loudly] said, "Snap. I am an …
[Pause slightly to allow audience to chime in answer]
ALLIGATOR. And I eat … wide mouth frogs.
[Make frog with hands and make him shake with fear.]

The Wide Mouth Frog said, "OH NO!" And he hopped on. From that time on, the wide mouth frog never again wandered in the wide, wide world.

Part VI

Other Handy Tales (Handkerchiefs, Napkins, Towels, and Other Props)

The Snooks Family

1. There were four people in the Snooks family. There was Papa Snooks. [Hold the napkin as a diamond. Touch the top corner for Papa Snooks.] There was Mama Snooks. [Rotate the napkin clockwise and touch the top corner for Mama Snooks.] There was Brother Snooks. [Rotate the napkin clockwise again and touch the top corner for Brother Snooks.] And there was Sister Snooks. [Rotate the napkin clockwise again and touch the top corner for Sister Snooks.]

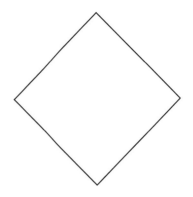

2. The Snooks family lived in a nice upstairs apartment. [Fold the napkin in half like a triangle. It will look like a rooftop.]

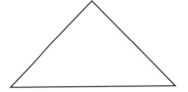

3. Each night, they would light a candle so they could see in the dark. [Fold the candle as indicated in the diagram as you are telling this part of the story. Then hold up the candle for the audience to see.]

 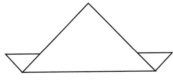 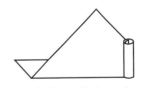 

Fold as indicated.   Turn away from you.   Roll napkin in and tuck in end to fasten.   Finished candle.

4. One night, it was time to go to bed. Mama Snooks couldn't find the candle snuffer so she asked Papa Snooks to blow out the candle. So Papa Snooks stood in front of the candle.

   He twisted his mouth and blew to the east. [Hold candle in front of you and blow out of the right corner of your mouth.]
   But the candle would not blow out. [With free hand, move index finger back and forth motioning "no."]

Finished candle.

5. Papa Snooks said, "Mama Snooks, why don't you blow out the candle?" So Mama Snooks stood in front of the candle.

    She twisted her mouth and blew to the west. [Hold candle in front of you and blow out of the left corner of your mouth.]
    But the candle would not blow out. [With free hand, move index finger back and forth motioning "no."]

6. Mama Snooks said, "Brother Snooks, why don't you blow out the candle?" So Brother Snooks stood in front of the candle.

    He twisted his mouth and blew to the north. [Hold candle in front of you and purse lips to blow air up.]
    But the candle would not blow out. [With free hand, move index finger back and forth motioning "no."]

7. Brother Snooks said, "Sister Snooks, why don't you blow out the candle? So Sister Snooks stood in front of the candle.

    She twisted her mouth and blew to the south. [Hold candle in front of you and purse lips to blow air down.]
    But the candle would not blow out. [With free hand, move index finger back and forth motioning "no."]

8. None of the Snooks family could blow out the candle! Sister Snooks looked out the window and saw a policeman downstairs. She said, "Papa, mama, there is a police man downstairs. Maybe he can help us." So Papa Snooks asked the policeman for help.

    The policeman came upstairs and stood in front of the candle.

    He held his mouth straight and blew straight ahead
    And the candle went out! [Hide candle behind back.]

9. Mama Snooks said, "Oh no! It's dark in here. We'll never be able to see to walk you out, Mr. Policeman." So she lit the candle. [Bring candle out again and hold in front of you.]

    Papa Snooks walked the policeman downstairs and waved goodbye. [Walk with candle in hand and wave goodbye.]

    When he returned upstairs, Mama Snooks said, "Papa Snooks, why don't you blow out the candle?" [Walk upstairs with the candle and face audience, holding candle in front of you.]

    Oh no! Here we blow again!!! [Begin blowing sequence again.]

The Mouse's Wedding
Japan

For this story, you will need two white handkerchiefs. You may begin the story with the mouse already made or delight the audience by creating the mouse as you tell the first paragraph of the story (you will make another mouse at the end of the story). One handkerchief will be used to portray Father Mouse and the other handkerchief will become the Sun, Cloud, Wind, and Wall. At the end, the second handkerchief is folded into another mouse. Be sure to practice your folding skills, as this story takes some time to learn. Once mastered, the changing shapes will astonish and captivate audiences.

1. Fold handkerchief into a triangle.

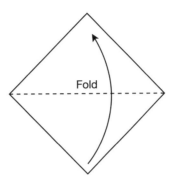 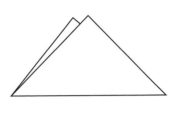

2. Fold in the points, overlapping slightly.

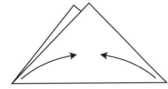 

3. Roll handkerchief from the bottom up. Flip it over.

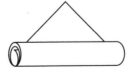 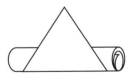

4. Bring each end toward each other, tucking one end into the other.

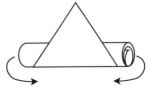

5. Fold the top point over and behind the tucked-in ends.

6. Roll both parts inwards (rolling over and over) until the ends emerge. One end will be the tail. The other end will become the head.

7. Open out one end and tie a knot to form a head with ears.

Long ago, there lived a rich mouse who had a beautiful daughter. His daughter had a handsome but poor suitor. The poor mouse wanted to marry the beautiful daughter but Father Mouse wanted his daughter to marry the mightiest creature in the world.

Create mouse and hold him in one hand. Move him around when he is "talking."

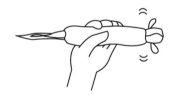

Father Mouse spoke to his wife. "Wife, our daughter has a common mouse for a suitor. But I cannot let my daughter marry unless she marries the mightiest creature in the world. Everyone knows the mightiest one is Mr. Sun."

Mother Mouse said, "Perhaps you should see him and ask him to marry our daughter." Father Mouse thought it was a good idea and set off to see the sun.

Make an upright fist with one hand. Lay the handkerchief over the top of the fist. Tuck handkerchief into hole at the top of the fist, forming a flower. This is the sun.

When he arrived, he bowed. [Have mouse bow before the sun.] "Good day, Mr. Sun. I want my daughter to marry the mightiest creature in the world. Since you bring light to the world, you must be the mightiest."

The Sun smiled, "I am flattered but I am afraid I am not the mightiest. When Mr. Cloud passes by, he covers my face. Therefore, he must be the mightiest."

Father Mouse thanked the Sun and continued on his journey.

Take the handkerchief and ball it in the fist, forming a cloud.

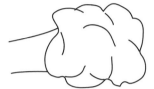

When he found the Cloud, he bowed. [Have mouse bow before the cloud.] "Good Day, Mr. Cloud. I want my daughter to marry the mightiest creature in the world. Since you cover Mr. Sun, you must be the mightiest."

The Cloud smiled, "I am flattered but I am afraid I am not the mightiest. When Mr. Wind comes near, he blows me across the sky. Therefore, he must be the mightiest."

Father Mouse thanked the Cloud and continued on his journey.

Hold handkerchief in one hand and move back and forth to signify wind.

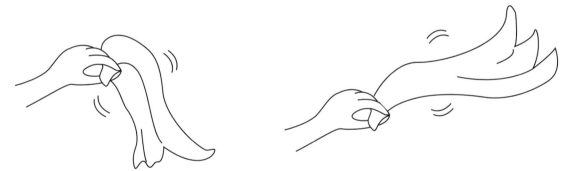

When he found the Wind, he bowed. [Have mouse bow before the wind.] "Good Day, Mr. Wind. I want my daughter to marry the mightiest creature in the world. Since you blow Mr. Cloud across the sky, you must be the mightiest."

The Wind smiled, "I am flattered but I am afraid I am not the mightiest. When I approach Mr. Wall, he stops me in my tracks. Therefore, he must be the mightiest."

Father Mouse thanked the Wind and continued on his journey.

Drape the handkerchief over one arm to create a "wall."

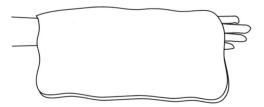

When he found the Wall, he bowed. [Have mouse bow before the wall.] "Good Day, Mr. Wall. I want my daughter to marry the mightiest creature in the world. Since you stop Mr. Wind in his tracks, you must be the mightiest."

The Wall smiled, "I am flattered but I am afraid I am not the mightiest. Do you see that hole in me? That hole is made by the mightiest creature around. He has the power to chew right through me!"

Father Mouse asked, "Honorable Mr. Wall, what creature has that kind of power?"

The Wall laughed. "Why, it's you, the mouse! You must be the mightiest creatures in the world!"

Father Mouse was surprised. He thanked the Wall and journeyed home.

He told his daughter to prepare for a wedding! [Begin folding the second mouse while telling the following part of the story.] Father Mouse discovered that the mightiest creature in the world was not the Sun, the mightiest creature in the world was not the Cloud, the mightiest creature in the world was not the Wind, the mightiest creature in the world was not the Wall. The mightiest creature in the world turned out to be a common … [allow audience to chime in the answer as you show the completed mouse] mouse!

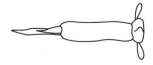

The mouse and the beautiful daughter were married. [Touch the two mice heads together and make a kissing sound.]

And they lived … happily ever after!

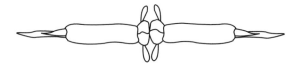

The Ugly Duckling
A Hans Christian Anderson Tale

Swan

1.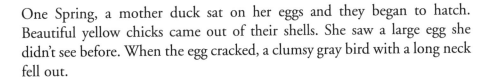

Lay full size towel flat.

2.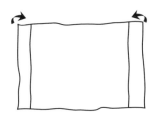

Fold ends of towel
to meet as shown.

3.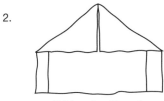

Roll outside edges to
meet as shown.

4.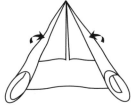

Ensure that the rolls
are tight and even.

5.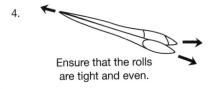

Make a "Z" fold to create
body and head.

One Spring, a mother duck sat on her eggs and they began to hatch. Beautiful yellow chicks came out of their shells. She saw a large egg she didn't see before. When the egg cracked, a clumsy gray bird with a long neck fell out.

The mother duck said, "What an ugly duckling!" The other chicks cried out,

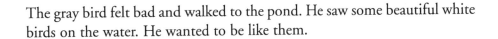

What an ugly duckling! What an ugly duckling!

The gray bird felt bad and walked to the pond. He saw some beautiful white birds on the water. He wanted to be like them.

The gray bird would come to the pond often to watch the beautiful white birds. Time passed and the gray bird grew bigger.

One day, he noticed his reflection in the water. He was no longer an ugly duckling! He turned into a beautiful white bird.

Some children saw him and came running to the pond. They cried out,

What a beautiful swan! What a beautiful swan!

We all transform with time.

Notes for telling: I like to use a gray hand towel for the ugly duckling. To make him look different, I wrap a rubber band around his beak and body, which makes him look like a gray duck. I use a white body towel to create the swan at the end. I tell as I fold and hold him up as I say "He turned into a beautiful white bird."

Bandana Man
A bandana folding tale

There was once an old woman [Fold bandana in half to form a triangle and wrap around head.]

1.

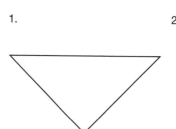

Fold bandana in half.

2.

who, more than anything wanted to have a baby. [With fold on the bottom, fold each corner to the opposite side so that it extends further than the body of the bandana. Then turn it over and tie the two corners, creating arms. Hold the baby bundle in your arms and rock back and forth.]

1.

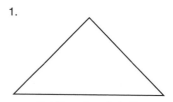

2.

3.

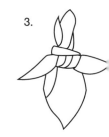

But alas, her wish did not come true. [Untie the arms and shake bandana out until it is a square once again]

Then one day, she remembered that she had a magic bandana. She said, "I am going to use that bandana to make a friend." She took out the bandana and spread it out on the table. Then she began rolling each side in until they met in the middle. She folded and folded and folded. She stretched the cloth and then she tied it. She held the cloth up and saw that she had a perfect little bandana man.

1.

2.

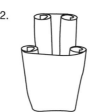

3.

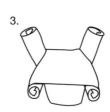

4.

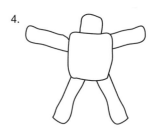

But remember, the bandana was magic. So when she was done, the bandana man began to run. As he ran along, he sang this song. [Tuck index finger of your right hand into the back of the bandana man and dance him around]

    "Run, run, run as fast as you can
    You can't catch me; I'm bandana man!"

He ran past the old woman into the forest. There he came upon an eight-legged creature. It was a … spider! [Form spider with left hand and wiggle fingers to create a "crawling" motion.]

The spider said, "Bandana man, I'm going to eat you up!" But the bandana man danced around and said, "Oh no you won't!" and he ran along as he sang this song.

    "Run, run, run as fast as you can
    You can't catch me; I'm bandana man!"

He ran past the spider further into the forest until he came upon a sssssssslithering ssssssssssnake! [Form a snake with left hand and "slither" around.]

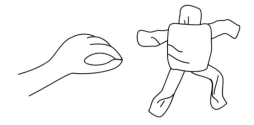

The snake said, "Bandana man, I'm going to eat you up!" But the bandana man danced around and said, "Oh no you won't!" and he ran along as he sang this song.

    "Run, run, run as fast as you can
    You can't catch me; I'm bandana man!"

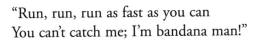

He ran past the snake further into the forest until he came to a rushing river. There, at the river's edge, was a fox! [Form a fox's head with left hand and open "mouth" to talk.] The fox said, "Bandana Man! Would you like to cross the river?"

Bandana Man said, "I don't know how to swim." [Make a swimming motion with hands.] Fox answered, "Hop on my back and I will swim you across." Bandana Man said, "Great idea!" He hopped on top of the fox's back. [Place bandana figure on top of fox's "back."]

But as the fox swam across, the water got deeper and deeper. Bandana Man had to climb on top of fox's nose. Then fox said, "Bandana Man, now I'm going to eat you up!" But Bandana Man said, "Oh no you won't!" Remember when I said the bandana was magic? Well, that Bandana Man wrapped his legs around fox's mouth and tied it shut. [Tie bandana legs around fox's mouth.] Fox tried to speak. [Mumble.]

Bandana Man said, "I'll let you go if you promise to take me to the other side." Fox nodded his yes and took Bandana Man to the other side of the river. Bandana Man untied Fox and began dancing away, leaving Fox far behind. He ran along as he sang this song. [Dance Bandana Man around.]

> "Run, run, run as fast as you can
> You can't catch me; I'm bandana man!"

Bandana Man outfoxed the fox!

The Frog and the Ox
A Balloon Tale based on An Aesop Fable

A little frog was nearly trampled by a big ox. The little frog hopped home to tell the biggest frog in the pond his story.
[With a balloon pump, blow up a green balloon to a small size. Attach a green scrunchie to it and slide it on your wrist. If you wish, you can give the frog a face. This can be done in advance.]

The little frog said, "It was a great big beast that nearly trampled me beneath its feet!"

The big frog, who was very vain, said, "Was he this big?" and he puffed himself up as much as he could.
[Using the balloon pump, blow up a green balloon to a large size.]

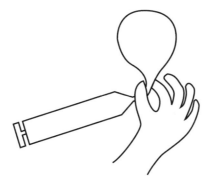

The little frog said,

> "Ribbit, Ribbit, Ribbit, he was bigger than that!
> Ribbit, Ribbit, Ribbit, he was fatter than fat!"

The big frog said, "Was he this big?" and he puffed himself up even bigger than before!
[Continue blowing up the balloon.]

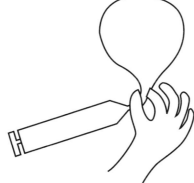

The little frog said,

"Ribbit, Ribbit, Ribbit, he was bigger than that!
Ribbit, Ribbit, Ribbit, he was fatter than fat!"

The big frog said, "Was he THIS big?" and he puffed himself up even bigger than before!
[Continue blowing up the balloon until it looks ready to burst.]

The big frog couldn't even reach half the ox's size. He tried in vain with all his might. He puffed himself up as big as the moon until, just like a balloon, he

POPPED!
[While saying this, prick the large frog balloon with a pin so it pops.]

The moral of this story is: If you try to be bigger than you are, you will explode with your own greatness.
[Face the little frog to the audience while saying this.]

Source Notes

"April Showers" is an original story. The cutting portion of the story was adapted from "Raindrop to Flower" in *Folded Paper Projects* (Monterey, CA: Evan-Moor Educational Publishers, 2000).

"Bandana Man" was adapted from "The Pancake" in *The Arbuthnot Anthology of Children's Literature*, 3rd ed., ed. Mark Taylor (Glenview, IL: Scott, Foresman and Company, 1970) and "Johnny Cake," in *English Fairy Tales* by Joseph Jacobs first published in 1890 and reprinted by Everyman's Library (New York: Alfred A. Knopf, 1993). The bandana cloth figure is a doll that was made by children in colonial times.

"Boy Who Drew Cats, The" was adapted from "The Boy Who Drew Cats" in *Japanese Fairy Tales* by Lafcadio Hearn (New York: Boni and Liveright, 1918), "The Boy Who Drew Cats" from *Mysterious Tales of Japan* by Rafe Martin (New York: G. P. Putnam's Sons, 1996), and "The Boy Who Drew Cats" in *Tales of Cats* by Pleasant DeSpain (Little Rock, AR: August House Publishers, 2003).

"Catching a Pest" is an original story. The idea for the story was inspired by my friend's name, Kat Mincz. The creation of the story was inspired by my friend Joe Wos, cartoonist and storyteller, who uses the alphabet to draw a rabbit. I wanted to create a story that used numbers to draw an animal. The mouse was the end result.

"Emperor's Dragon, The" is an original draw and tell story inspired by a Chinese folktale called "Drawing the Dragon," which I first saw in *Storytelling Professionally* by Harlynne Geisler (Englewood, CO: Libraries Unlimited, 1997).

"Emperor's New Clothes, The" is liberally adapted from "The Emperor's New Clothes" by Hans Christian Anderson in *Classic Library: Fairy Tales Hans Christian Anderson* (London, England: Anness Publishing Limited, 1995).

"Fox Chases Bunny," is an original story using shoestring tying as inspiration. I thought storytelling would be a fun way to teach children how to tie their shoes. In addition, once they learn the story, they would always have a story to make and take.

"Frog and the Ox, The" is adapted from "The Frog and the Ox" in *Aesop's Fables*, selected and adapted by Jack Zipes (New York: The Penguin Group, 1992) and "The Frogs and the Ox" in *The Aesop for Children* (New York: Scholastic, 1994). Using a balloon to tell the story was inspired by my friend, Gale Criswell, youth services coordinator for the State Library of Louisiana. She used a pink balloon to portray a pig in a different story.

"Gary's Wings" is an original story. My father was a jet engine mechanic for the Navy. He taught me how to make pilot's wings and rings out of dollar bills, which was the inspiration for this story. This story was written for my brother, Gary.

"Girl Who Used her Wits, The" was adapted from "The Young Head of the Family" in *Best-Loved Folktales* selected by Joanna Cole (New York: Bantam Books by Doubleday, 1982), "The Youngest, Wisest Wife" in *Around the World in 80 Tales* by Nicola Baxter (Leicester, England: Armadillo Books, 2002), and "The Young Head of the Cheng Family" from *Tales the People Tell in China* by Robert Wyndham (New York: Julian Messner, A Division of Simon & Schuster, 1971).

"Grandma's Party" is an original tale based on the concept of the Russian Matryoshka nesting dolls. I learned this note-folding technique in elementary school as a way to pass notes to classmates, possibly without the teacher noticing. Of course, someone always got caught!

"Great Pirate Adventure, The" is an original story. I was inspired to create a pirate story from the newspaper hats and boats I learned to fold as a child. In this story, I wanted to use a single sheet of newspaper to tell the story. When my youngest daughter was four years old, she taught me how to make the "tree." She learned it from a PBS television program called *Zoom.*

"Joseph Had an Overcoat" was adapted from *Joseph Had a Little Overcoat* by Simms Taback (New York: Penguin Putnam Books for Young Readers, 1999). I first heard this story from friend and fellow storyteller, John Lehon. I developed this cut and tell for a series of Louisiana summer reading workshops.

"King's Advisor, The" is an original story. I learned the book folding trick many years ago and developed the story around the idea of creating a book.

"Magic Star, The" is an original story. I learned the paper trick of cutting a star out of a single sheet of paper with one cut while developing stories for the Louisiana Summer Reading workshops several years ago.

"Magic Story Starter, The" is adapted from "cootie catchers" or "paper fortune tellers" from this popular playground game of my childhood.

"Mouse's Wedding, The" was adapted from a Japanese Kamishibai play titled "The Mouse's Wedding" by Seishi Horio (New York: Twinkle Tales for Kids, 1997), *The Mouse Bride* by Joy Crowley (New York: Scholastic, 1995), "The Beautiful Mouse Girl" in *Japanese Folktales* by James E. O'Donnell (Caldwell, ID: The Caxton Printers, 1958), and "Nezumi No Yomeiri" from Folk Legends of Japan Web site http://web-japan.org/kidsweb/folk.html. When I was a little girl, my grandfather showed me how to fold a mouse out of a handkerchief. That became the basis of the inspiration for this story.

"Mr. Wiggle and Mr. Waggle" is a traditional hand tale. Storytellers around the world use this tale in many variants. I believe I learned this story from storyteller Carolyn Greene in New Orleans.

"Papa's Teepee" was adapted with permission from "The Chief's New Home" by Margie Willis Clary. I first learned the story from Karen Chace who learned it from Suzette Hawkins. Suzette learned the story from Margie Willis Clary, the tale's originator. Margie kindly gave me permission to adapt and retell the story.

"Pesky Skeeter, The" is an original story that was developed for my "Creepy Crawler Critter Tales" program about bugs. It uses a string figure called "The Mosquito."

"Pilot's Wheel, The" is an original story. It uses a paper trick called "The Anchor and Ship's Wheel."

"Royal Paper Puzzle, The" is an original story. Walking through a sheet of paper is an old trick I learned many years ago, although I can't remember where (Girl Scouts?). I developed the rest of the story and paper tricks to follow a folktale style of story in which a king issues a challenge or a puzzle.

"Snooks Family, The" was adapted from a version told to me by my friend Gale Criswell, children's librarian and youth services consultant for the State Library of Louisiana and "The Twist-Mouth Family" in *From Sea to Shining Sea*, compiled by Amy L. Cohn (New York: Scholastic, 1993). The napkin folding was inspired by restaurant napkin folding.

"Stubborn Turnip, The" was adapted from *The Gigantic Turnip* by Alexei Tolstoy (Cambridge, MA: Barefoot Books, 2006) and *The Enormous Potato* by Aubrey Davis (Kids Can Press, 1999). The string part of the story uses a string figure called "The Worm."

"Ugly Duckling, The" was adapted from childhood memories of the story and "The Ugly Little Duck" in *Andersen's Fairy Tales*, by Hans Christian Andersen (New York: Anness Publishing Limited, 1995). The towel folding was inspired by cruise line towel folding.

"Wide Mouth Frog, The" is adapted from a traditional tale called "The Wide Mouth Frog." Over the years, I have heard many storytellers tell this story. My favorite version, and the one that inspired my adaptation, is from storyteller and musician Dan Keding. More than 10 years ago, Dan taught me how to make a frog with my hands to accompany the tale.

"Worm, The" is an original story using the string figure called "The Worm."

Resources

Here are some print resources that will help you in creating your own handmade tales.

Darsie, Richard. *String Games.* New York: Sterling Publishing Company, 2003.

Emberly, Ed. *Ed Emberly's Drawing Books of Animals.* New York: Little, Brown and Company, 1970.

Folder, Alan. *Paper Tricks.* New York: Tangerine Press, 2000.

Frorath, Gunther. *Cat's Cradle and the World's Best String Games.* New York: Mud Puddle Books, 2005.

Fujita, Hiroko, and Fran Stallings. *Stories to Play With.* Little Rock, AR: August House Publishers, 1999.

Johnson, Anne Akers. *The Buck Book.* Palo Alto, CA: Klutz, 1993.

Johnson, Anne Akers. *Cat's Cradle.* Palo Alto, CA: Klutz, 1993.

Pellowski, Anne. *Drawing Stories from Around the World.* Westport, CT: Libraries Unlimited, 2005.

Pellowski, Anne. *The Family Storytelling Handbook.* New York: Macmillan Publishing Company, 1987.

Spence, Elizabeth. *Newspaper Fun.* Baton Rouge, LA: Baton Rouge Advocate, 1985.

Index

About the Author

DIANNE DE LAS CASAS is an award-winning storyteller and author who tours internationally presenting programs, training teachers and librarians, and conducting workshops and artist residencies. Her performances, dubbed "traditional folklore gone fun," are full of energetic audience participation. Visit her Web site at www.storyconnection.net.